Releasing Your Story

A PATH TO REDISCOVERY

ANN MARIE BRYANT

outskirtspress
DENVER, COLORADO

Outskirts Press, Inc.
http://www.outskirtspress.com

ISBN: 978-1-4787-1913-7

Outskirts Press and the "OP" logo are trademarks belonging to Outskirts Press, Inc.

PRINTED IN THE UNITED STATES OF AMERICA

Contents

CHAPTER 1

If You Are Not Growing, You Are Dying.

You are already taking a step in the right direction. By deciding to change your story, you are moving toward a life with no boundaries. You will free yourself to pursue whatever is in your heart and more importantly once and for all believe you can attain your dream. Once you learn the process of changing your story, you can continue to work on your entire belief system and let go of what is simply not true. You will have the capability to constantly improve yourself because you will be looking at life with a new set of eyes, ones that see the possibility and goodness that lie all around you.

You probably already have in mind what you feel you are lacking in your life. However, you may not quite understand why your dreams and goals seem unattainable. This workbook will show you the countless tricks the mind plays on us and how to overcome these illusions, which will greatly improve your life.

Let's get started!

Past

Who were you as a child? Describe yourself—your thoughts, appearance, and what you liked to do in as much detail as possible.

_____

_____

_____

_____

_____

_____

_____

_____

_____

_____

_____

_____

Present

Who do you feel you are today? Describe yourself—your thoughts,
appearance, and what you like to do in as much detail as possible.

_____

_____

_____

_____

_____

_____

_____

_____

_____

_____

_____

Let's Go a Little Further.

Make a list of 3 times when you were truly happy. Go back in time and feel that happiness. What was the situation? Who was around you? What were the sights, smells, and feelings surrounding this experience? What were the thoughts going through your head?

#1 _____

_____

_____

_____

_____

_____

_____

_____

_____

_____

#2

#3 _____

_____

_____

_____

_____

_____

_____

_____

_____

_____

_____

_____

_____

_____

Now make a list of 3 times when you were truly unhappy. How did it feel? What was the situation? Who was around you? What were the sights, smells, and feelings surrounding this experience? What were the thoughts going through your head?

#1 _____

_____

_____

_____

_____

_____

_____

_____

_____

_____

_____

_____

#2 _____

_____

_____

_____

_____

_____

_____

_____

_____

_____

_____

_____

_____

_____

#3 _____

_____

_____

_____

_____

_____

_____

_____

_____

_____

_____

_____

_____

_____

_____

Recalling these situations may lead you to your story, a tale you developed after a painful incident happened to protect yourself from feeling that way again. For example, a child may have been on a team and the score was tied. The child had the opportunity to score a point and win the game for his team but missed. Everyone was upset. They gave him dirty looks and said unkind things to him. He was humiliated and crushed by this experience and just wanted to go home. The story that might develop from the situation is "I'm horrible at sports." Now fast-forward a bit and he is at a family picnic. Someone asks if he wants to play (fill in the blank) and he immediately says "no" because he is reminded of his story "I'm horrible at sports."

You can see how these stories impact you and your future. This person could have enjoyed a friendly game with his family and had some laughs but instead, he chose to sit on the sidelines and observe. This is what your stories basically do, they keep you on the sidelines of life, keeping you from taking advantage of all of the opportunities that present themselves.

When you thought of your happy times it felt great. I am sure you felt love, joy, and pure contentment that you wish would never end. You now have the opportunity to open yourself up to experience this kind of happiness again in your life by letting go of your stories.

CHAPTER 2

What Is Your Story?

Your story is something you have determined about yourself based on something you experienced, whether it is an extremely painful event or a simple occurrence that took place. When you look back at an event without it being a great memory you simply want to relive, there is likelihood there is a story attached to that memory.

For example, I had a conversation with my mother my freshman year of high school. We were sitting in the front seat of her car and we were talking about college, careers, and what I should be when I grew up. I remember my mom saying to me, "Why don't you just be a stewardess (flight attendant nowadays), then you can meet a man and travel the world for free?"

I remember this conversation so vividly, and to anyone else this may have seemed like a simple and harmless suggestion. However, what I took away was a huge and highly damaging story about myself. What I heard was:

1) You are not smart enough to go to college.

2) You do not have the capability of taking care of yourself so you better find a man to do it.

So ultimately my most damaging story was:

You are really not that smart and you better marry someone to take care of you.

In these next pages, I invite you to explore some of your memories to help you determine what one of your stories is.

When looking back at one of your three painful experiences you described on the previous pages, what "lessons" did you walk away with? What did you feel you learned about yourself?

#1 _____

_____

_____

_____

_____

_____

_____

_____

_____

#2 _____

_____

_____

_____

#3

Can you think of any other incidents, big or small, where a "lesson" may have been acquired?

_____

_____

_____

_____

_____

_____

_____

_____

_____

_____

_____

Did you gather a general feeling about yourself or your abilities as a result of any of these experiences? If so, what are they?

_____

_____

_____

_____

_____

_____

_____

_____

_____

_____

_____

_____

What is your story?

_____

_____

_____

_____

_____

_____

_____

_____

_____

_____

_____

_____

_____

_____

_____

_____

_____

_____

_____

_____

_____

_____

_____

I'm so glad you have started on this journey. By letting go of faulty beliefs, you will open up space in your heart to let light in: positivity, passion, and joy. By learning to let go of your story, you will find the key to open doors in areas such as gaining a sense of purpose, finding and attaining your passions, attaining your goals, and so much more. This is truly a powerful process! I'm delighted you have decided to keep growing.

CHAPTER 3

Whatever You Want to Create, First Starts in the Mind.

Everything starts in the mind. You have a thought, then you have the choice to execute it. "Oh, ice cream, that sounds good." Then you find yourself at the freezer getting yourself some ice cream. Think about the pen or pencil you are using to complete this workbook. It was someone's idea, then they acted on it and made it a reality.

You have thousands of thoughts each and every day, but right now you are going to use those thoughts to dream big. What do you want out of life? Pretend you are a kid again. Remember those dreams? Who do you want to be when you grow up? What are you passionate about? Let your mind wander free as you complete the following pages.

Let's Look at Your Future.

Who do you want to be? Think about career and work.

_____

_____

_____

_____

_____

_____

_____

_____

_____

_____

_____

_____

How do you want to feel about yourself? Think about your health and fitness.

_____

_____

_____

_____

_____

_____

_____

_____

_____

_____

_____

_____

What hobbies do you want to actively pursue? What would you like to include in your fun and recreation?

_____

_____

_____

_____

_____

_____

_____

_____

_____

_____

_____

_____

What would your ideal home life look like?

_____

_____

_____

_____

_____

_____

_____

_____

_____

_____

_____

_____

_____

What would your financial situation look like?

_____

_____

_____

_____

_____

_____

_____

_____

_____

_____

_____

_____

How would you describe your relationships with others?

_____

_____

_____

_____

_____

_____

_____

_____

_____

_____

_____

_____

_____

What would your family relationships be like?

_____

_____

_____

_____

_____

_____

_____

_____

_____

_____

_____

_____

What passions do you want to actively pursue?

_____

_____

_____

_____

_____

_____

_____

_____

_____

_____

_____

_____

_____

How do you want others to perceive you?

_____

_____

_____

_____

_____

_____

_____

_____

_____

_____

_____

_____

_____

What story do you need to let go of in order to attain what you envision?

_____

_____

_____

_____

_____

_____

_____

_____

_____

_____

_____

_____

_____

CHAPTER 4

Why Is Releasing Your Story So Important?

Changing your story is the key to unlocking your true potential and achieving transformation. Think about who you would be without those negative perceptions about yourself. What kind of relationships would you have? What would you wear? What would you feel free to do and pursue in life? Would you wait around until others came to your rescue or would you take charge of your own life and stop being a victim?

You have the power and capability to do so much in your life. Just believe in those positive thoughts and the rest should follow.

We have looked into who you were as a child and what made you happy; we also looked into negative experiences which may have led to your story. Furthermore, we delved into who you want to be when this process is over and what you want out of specific areas of your life.

You've got one shot. There is no "Wait, can I do that again? I wasn't quite ready the first time." Like it or not, this is it! Aren't you tired of passing up opportunities and not living life to its fullest?

Let's keep going on this journey!

Pain of Not Doing "It"

What will be the outcome if you don't do what your heart desires? How would you feel?

_____

_____

_____

_____

_____

_____

_____

_____

_____

_____

_____

Pretend you are an outsider looking in at someone who just sits on the outskirts of an event, dance, conversation, party, game, people having fun, etc.... You can tell they would really like to join in but they just sit instead. What would you say to them? How would you encourage them to join the fun?

_____

_____

_____

_____

_____

_____

_____

_____

_____

_____

_____

What if someone told you those exact same words? Could you take your own advice? What is the worst that could happen if you were to follow your advice?

_____

_____

_____

_____

_____

_____

_____

_____

_____

_____

_____

_____

How could you survive if the worst-case scenario did happen?

_____

_____

_____

_____

_____

_____

_____

_____

_____

_____

_____

_____

No one wants to feel they lived a lifetime of regrets. We all had moments where the "should of's/could of's" have crept on us. Don't let those moments accumulate to where they outnumber the good memories we hold onto forever. Give yourself a chance to really start living by letting go of your story.

CHAPTER 5

What Is Your Legacy?

We all have loved ones and friends; what kind of memories are you leaving behind for them? We often think we are our own entity, that no one really cares what I do or what I do doesn't really make a difference. But it is really quite the opposite. Our life is like a pebble being tossed into a still pond: we cause ripples, and we affect others. You may have heard the saying "don't cause any waves," but what if those waves are of joy, creating beauty, or helping others? Like it or not our lives affect others; however, **how** you affect other people's lives is up to you.

You are going to give yourself the advantage of pretending you have already lived your life. Will it be a joyous life or humdrum? The choice is yours.

Let's begin!

Write your biography based on how you are living now. What would your life look like if you continue the path you are on now? Include your life as a child, teen, adult, and elder. Make sure to include testimonials and stories from loved ones and friends.

_____

_____

_____

_____

_____

_____

_____

_____

_____

_____

_____

Rewrite your biography based on all of your goals and dreams being fulfilled. What would you like your biography to look like? Include your life as a child, teen, adult, and elder. Make sure to include testimonials and stories from loved ones and friends.

_____

_____

_____

_____

_____

_____

_____

_____

_____

_____

_____

_____

CHAPTER 6

How Do You Eat An Elephant?
One Bite at a Time.

To live the life we want does not magically happen all at once. We need to break it all down into pieces. Breaking things into pieces not only makes things manageable but also helps you from feeling overwhelmed from the whole transformational process.

By breaking things down into pieces, you give yourself the opportunity to make some kind of progress every day. You simply look at your list and choose one thing. Maybe one day you have quite a bit of time and feel ambitious, so you choose a larger task. Maybe it is a hectic day and all you have time for is a phone call. The choice is yours, but at least you have a variety of things to choose from and you can make some progress every day.

Let's make your goals small and specific.

Glance at your life as it is now and jot down what you do not want to appear in your life anymore.

_____

_____

_____

_____

_____

_____

Again, take a glance at your life and jot down what you do want more of in your life.

_____

_____

_____

_____

_____

_____

These two exercises should have gotten your "juices" flowing. Now I want you to really dig deep and examine your life and answer the following questions.

What I do not want to appear in my life anymore:

_____

_____

_____

_____

_____

_____

_____

_____

_____

_____

_____

_____

What I do want to appear in my life:

_____

_____

_____

_____

_____

_____

_____

_____

_____

_____

_____

_____

What are my top 5 goals or passions?

#1 _____

_____

_____

_____

_____

#2 _____

_____

_____

_____

_____

#3 _____

_____

_____

_____

_____

_____

#4 _____

_____

_____

_____

_____

_____

#5 _____

_____

_____

_____

_____

_____

Now that you have specific goals or things that you want in your life, you can begin to say "yes" to them. In the same token, now that you have identified what you DO NOT want to appear in your life, you can make a conscious effort to steer clear of those situations.

CHAPTER 7

Start Living Life And Not Just Going Through the Motions.

Many live life by the "sidelines," playing it safe, not wanting to cause any waves; good or bad and life has become a routine. You get up at the same time, grab a cup of coffee, go to work, eat, and sleep. There are not many variables. Many of us may have developed a negative rut and don't even know it. Have you ever driven somewhere and do not know how you got there? This may be a symptom. A negative rut is when little thought goes into your actions. You just do because that is what you have always done. This is extremely dangerous because precious time is wasted without you even knowing it. You may find you are in a negative rut on your birthday or New Year's Eve when you look back at the year and say, "Where has the time gone?" but the point is the time has gone and there are no do-overs. The reality is more time has passed where you did not actively pursue your goals or dreams to the point where they may have become a faint memory.

Your story can be a part of your negative rut because it keeps you conditioned to feel you are less than worthy or capable. Your story covers up fear—fear of being ridiculed, fear of letting others down, fear of looking like a fool, and I could go on and on. So you develop a story to protect yourself from feeling that pain again.

Your story may sound like:

If I didn't do _____ this would never have happened. *Or*

I shouldn't have done _____ because this is now happening. I know I'll never do that again.

A story that covers up fear may help you in the moment, but will definitely hurt you in the long run. Now is the time to be honest with yourself as to why you have not pursued what you wanted. I know this may not be easy to admit, but it is necessary in completely letting go of the negative story you have built in your mind.

Now we all can definitely learn from experience; however, it becomes a problem when you find yourself living life in a negative way because of one incident. In order to start living "out loud," take a stand on something or follow the song in your heart. Now is the time to start really living, not simply breathing, eating, sleeping, and doing activities on autopilot. Start making decisions, start questioning things, and start choosing in favor of you.

Let's begin!

What have you always wanted to do but have not because it seems impossible to accomplish? You may look back at your goals or passions and what you want more of in your life if you feel stuck.

_____

_____

_____

_____

_____

_____

_____

_____

_____

_____

_____

_____

What is the fear surrounding why you have not fulfilled that goal or dream?

_____

_____

_____

_____

_____

_____

_____

_____

_____

Sometimes we all get "be careful of what you wish for" syndrome. The mind may start to get overloaded with all of the problems we may face if we were to get that dream job or move to a new house, etc.... We may in fact create so many negative scenarios that the positives get completely overlooked. Now is the time to zone in on what may be holding you back.

Can you think of anything positive that would happen by not accomplishing your goal? What do you gain?

_____

_____

_____

_____

_____

_____

_____

_____

_____

_____

_____

_____

_____

_____

_____

_____

_____

_____

_____

_____

By identifying these underlying fears, you can address what else may be keeping you from achieving your goal or passion. After identifying the fear, perhaps you may want to reevaluate what you really want or work on ways to tame and ultimately delete that fear from your memory.

If you are reconsidering your goal or passion, hold tight before you make any decisions because the next section may be exactly what you need to make your dream seem more like a possibility again.

Downsizing May Be the Key.

Perhaps you are not ready to be the big boss or get another degree…
however, there are steps you can take that will get you closer to your
goal without feeling overwhelmed. If you want to go back to school
and earn a degree, instead of enrolling as a full- or part-time student,
you may just take one class and see how it goes. Think of these steps
as getting into a cold swimming pool; some may dive right in, like
enrolling full time, but others may need a little time to get used to the
water. Do you go in waist deep like enrolling part time, or do you dip
your toe in and take one class? The choice is yours, but at least you
are moving forward toward your goal or dream. Once you take those
initial steps, you may find what you thought would be scary or negative is actually not a big deal at all.

What things do you feel comfortable doing that would get you moving toward your ultimate goal?

Do not stay in the trap where regret may seem more appealing than rejection. Again, most of us have been conditioned to think this way; just go through life and don't cause any waves.

Set yourself free from the trance and no longer settle. Actively take steps toward owning your dream house, attracting that perfect partner, having a wonderful career, and so on and so forth. The sky is the limit!

CHAPTER 8

This Is About YOU!

After looking at your childhood and determining what one of your stories is, you had an opportunity to look into your future and determine what you ultimately want out of life.

You found out the importance of changing your story and how you could most likely endure any consequences of "going for it."

After reading your biography of what your life may look like if you continue on the path you are on and the biography of what your life may look like if you decide to live life to its fullest, you found your ultimate goal may need to be broken up into baby steps to achieve. I hope you have decided to start really living life and not just going through the motions because this is about YOU!

We all have thoughts and dreams about what our perfect life would be like. The perfect house, job, neighborhood, friends, social functions we would be attending, and what our bankbook would look like, etc....

Take inventory of what your ideal life would encompass. Describe everything your ideal life would have in it. Pretend you just woke up in the softest, most comfortable bed possible and you are getting ready to put your feet on the floor. Think of all of the things you would be doing that day. What would you be wearing? What kind of car would you be driving? Take a good look at your surroundings. What kind of kitchen would you go to for your orange juice or coffee? Where would you drink it? Perhaps you would be going to the club to dine? Think of all the things you would encounter in one day of your dream life.

_____

_____

_____

_____

_____

_____

_____

_____

Now take the time to describe yourself while living your dream life. What would you look like? How would you feel about your appearance? How would you feel on the inside about the day ahead? How would you feel when you look around and see all of the beautiful things you have? How would you feel when you look at your bankbook? How would you feel when you think about future plans? How would you feel physically? How would you feel about your relationships with friends and family? Really go deep.

_____

_____

_____

_____

_____

_____

_____

_____

_____

_____

Now take inventory of what your life encompasses now. Picture yourself in bed getting ready to put your feet on the floor. Think of all of the things you will be doing that day. Think of what you will be wearing, what kind of car you will be driving. Take a good look at your surroundings. What kind of kitchen will you go to for your orange juice or coffee? Where will you drink it? Think of all the things you will be encountering.

Now take the time to describe yourself as you are in this scenario. What do you look like? How do you feel about your appearance? How do you feel on the inside about the day ahead? How do you feel when you look around at your things? How do you feel when you look at your bankbook? How do you feel when you think about future plans? How do you feel physically? How do you feel about your relationships with friends and family? Really go deep.

_____

_____

_____

_____

_____

_____

_____

_____

_____

_____

Everyone has positive and negative aspects about themselves and about in life in general. This is not an exercise to make you feel inferior or hopeless. The intent, however, is to see where you are. We want to pull forward areas of your life that you would not want to change no matter what and areas of your life that you would like to improve upon because ultimately this is about YOU. We all need to feel a sense of importance. We need to know we are here for a reason and not just floundering through life.

With that being said, compare both scenarios and what you wrote about each. Choose two areas you love having in your life and two areas which you would like to improve upon.

Two areas you love in your life as they are now:

_____

_____

_____

_____

_____

_____

_____

_____

Two areas in your life you would like to improve upon:

_____

_____

_____

_____

_____

_____

_____

_____

_____

_____

_____

_____

_____

_____

_____

_____

_____

_____

_____

_____

_____

_____

It is very rare that focusing on just one part of your life will bring you happiness. It's okay to focus on yourself; however, if you stay on track but miss your daughter's recital and feel absolutely awful, it may become a problem. It's okay to skip your activity for something important that cannot be rescheduled. Be happy and be there for your family and the things that count; just don't forget yourself by the wayside.

CHAPTER 9

Stop Spinning Your Wheels.

Turning your pain into motivation can be a positive; however, there may be other items lurking in the background that can also negatively impact your quest. Have you had the best intention to lose weight but find yourself eating chips or ice cream not even a week into your diet? This may be one isolated incident, but it may also be a way of life that needs to be changed. These self-sabotaging habits may make you happy at that moment or keep you from feeling uncomfortable, but ultimately these habits keep putting you further and further away from the goals you would like to attain. So you are going to do some exploring and get rid of these negative ways once and for all.

You Are a Diva!

You are a diva and I hope this is not news to you. Do you realize how wonderful you really are? You need to be able to toot your own horn because if you don't, who will? If you feel uneasy saying you are a diva, pay close attention.

Do you realize it takes over 15,000 hours of class time in order to earn a high-school diploma? If you are a parent, do you realize all of the "hats" you need to wear? You have to be a therapist, nurse, secretary, cook, counselor, fashion coordinator, personal shopper, nutritionist, taxi driver, private investigator, among other things to parent. Just to manage a household is a tremendous feat. You have accomplished things others would be amazed at. You may even hear it from time to time yet dismiss it as "Oh, it was nothing."

Take inventory and write down the things you are grateful for in each of the following sections:

Family, friends, and pets; you can also include groups as well. State who they are and why you are grateful for them.

_____

_____

_____

_____

_____

_____

Places you have loved or love. It can include places that give you peace or a good meal. Anywhere that makes you feel good. State these places and why you are grateful for them.

_____

_____

_____

_____

_____

_____

_____

_____

_____

_____

_____

_____

Things you value. These are the material things that bring you joy. It could be something like a pair of jeans that hug in all the right places or a vase because flowers always look so pretty in it.

_____

_____

_____

_____

_____

_____

_____

_____

_____

_____

_____

_____

_____

You might say "What is the point of this?" but it's always good to be thankful for what you have. Sometimes we get so caught up in what we do not have, how things would be so much better "if only..." that we overlook what is staring us right in the face.

Look at each section you have completed:

Family, friends, pets, and groups you love
Places you love
Things you love

State what part you played in bringing all of these things you love into your life. Did you initially find that favorite restaurant or were you the first to say "hi" when you met your best friend? Go through your lists.

_____

_____

_____

_____

_____

_____

_____

_____

Now let's really take a look inward. What do others admire in you?

_____

_____

_____

_____

_____

_____

_____

_____

_____

_____

_____

_____

What do others thank you for?

_____

_____

_____

_____

_____

_____

_____

_____

_____

_____

_____

_____

_____

Now ask one of your closest friends what your best attributes are and why they are your friend.

_____

_____

_____

_____

_____

_____

_____

_____

_____

_____

_____

_____

It's funny how you can become your own worst critic. You may think you are so much less than what you actually are, and until you claim yourself as being valuable you risk playing into what you perceive as reality, which is often a far cry from the truth.

Now that you have a clearer picture of who you really are and all of the gifts and talents you possess, take another look: Name one thing you wanted to complete but did not?

_____

_____

_____

_____

_____

_____

_____

_____

_____

_____

What was going through your head at the time you were faced with
the decision to do it or not?

_____

_____

_____

_____

_____

How did you feel after making the decision not to do it?

_____

_____

_____

_____

_____

How do you feel looking back at it now? Go deep with this.

_____

_____

_____

_____

_____

_____

_____

_____

_____

_____

_____

_____

If you could go back and experience it now, would you? If yes, what made you change your mind?

_____

_____

_____

_____

_____

_____

_____

_____

_____

_____

_____

_____

If not, what's stopping you?

_____

_____

_____

_____

_____

_____

_____

_____

_____

_____

_____

Is there a story connected to what is stopping you? If so, what is it?

_____

_____

_____

_____

_____

_____

_____

_____

_____

_____

_____

_____

_____

_____

Be kind to yourself and let go of the harsh critiques. It is time to advocate for yourself and focus on your positive attributes. It is okay to toot your own horn every once in a while. Be proud of who you are and know that you have so much to offer the world. Believe in yourself and do not be surprised when you see yourself attain one goal after the other.

CHAPTER 10

It's Not Your Fault.

Sometimes even though there may be a story attached to why you are not willing to pursue something, it may also be a feeling of responsibility. You may have taken responsibility for events you really had no control over.

What is usually overlooked is there was a likelihood of that incident happening with or without your involvement. Stop taking the blame for things you had no control over. It's time to move on and stop being the martyr! I promise whatever is going to happen is going to happen regardless if you continue to worry about it or not. Focus on the good you are doing in your life. Stop focusing on the negative; it does more harm than good.

Look back at your goals on page 62. Do you feel these goals are achievable? I hope you answered "yes" because guess what? They are! How do I know this? I know it because somebody has already done them. Whenever I feel overwhelmed I think about this simple fact. Suppose I want to lose fifteen pounds. Guess what, somebody already lost that amount of weight and more, so if they can do it why can't I?

I will never forget giving birth to my 8 lbs. 11 oz. son without an epidural. I was in such pain towards the end that I literally thought I was going to die. At that time a nurse came to my bedside and said, "Ann Marie, you are neither the first nor the last woman to do this, focus!" I have to admit I was not a happy camper having heard that statement, but it is something I go back to time and time again. I'm not the only one to pursue XYZ and others have succeeded, so why can't I? I encourage you to make up your own mantra that will remind you of how anything is possible. Write it down.

_____

_____

_____

_____

_____

_____

_____

_____

I also encourage you to make note cards of your mantra. Keep one with you and post others throughout your home and workplace so you do not forget anything is possible.

Now write your top 5 goals or passions.

#1 _____

_____

_____

_____

_____

#2 _____

_____

_____

_____

#3 _____

_____

_____

_____

_____

_____

#4 _____

_____

_____

_____

_____

_____

#5 _____

_____

_____

_____

_____

_____

_____

I also encourage you to make note cards of your goals or passions as well. Keep a note card with you and post the others throughout your home as a reminder of what you are going for and moving closer toward.

Release yourself from responsibility and lift the weight off of your shoulders. If something happened in the past, there is nothing you can do about it. The event already happened, it is gone, and there are no re-dos. Please stop beating yourself up over something that will never change. Make amends and move on.

CHAPTER 11

Releasing Your Story.

Once you change your story, you will look at information in a completely different way because your thoughts will not be based on fear. Think of how differently you will process what you encounter. Instead of being someone that is constantly doubting themselves or looking for the negatives in every situation, you can take what comes at you, and run with it or dismiss it, instead of letting it eat you up inside. Your life will not seem so out of control because changing your story will help you take charge and be honest with yourself. You can make decisions based on facts, not beliefs.

In order to really transform your perceptions, you must commit to do what it takes to make that change. We all have obstacles and barriers, but the difference between someone wanting to fulfill their dream and someone actually doing it is their actions because let's face it, talk is cheap. Once you are motivated and confident that change is possible, you are ready to make some real progress.

What do you stand to lose by not changing your story? Think of your biography based on how you are living now and go deeper with it. Relate it specifically to your five goals or passions.

_____

_____

_____

_____

_____

_____

_____

_____

_____

_____

_____

_____

Now it's time to release yourself from the faulty perception your story has given you. Write down in full detail the actual events surrounding your story. Who was present? What was actually said during the conversation? This is not the time to infer. Pretend you are a journalist just stating the facts.

_____

_____

_____

_____

_____

_____

_____

_____

_____

_____

_____

_____

Now go back to the event as yourself and write down your perception of what happened.

_____

_____

_____

_____

_____

_____

_____

_____

_____

_____

_____

_____

Next, write a letter to yourself giving yourself permission to release those negative feelings surrounding that event. You may want to read the journalist version of the event so you might gain insight as to what actually happened versus what you felt happened.

You may start out, "Dear , you have my permission to set yourself free from the hurtful misperceptions you have been carrying around all of this time…."

Try to address why you believe the story evolved the way it did. Also, address the fact that it was just trying to protect you from further harm. Send love and appreciation toward the story but also recognize that it is no longer needed.

_____

_____

_____

_____

_____

_____

_____

_____

_____

Now that you have acknowledged the fact that you no longer need your story to protect you, I hope you feel as if a weight has been lifted from your shoulders. You have released your story, and you may feel lighter and even have a more positive outlook on life in general. Take the time and think of all of the possibilities that lie ahead of you. You may even say to yourself, "I am no longer (fill in whatever your false perception was)," and take note of how it feels.

You are on your way!

CHAPTER 12

Setting Others Free.

You have accomplished quite a bit thus far. When you started on this journey, you found the importance of thinking positively because whatever you create first starts in the mind. Next, you focused on how your life affects others and why it is so important to release your story. You then found ways to break down your big goals and passions into smaller, more attainable pieces to avoid feeling overwhelmed. After that, you went on to notice how talented you really are and take note of all of the good things in your life. Finally, you acknowledged you no longer need your story to protect you and released it.

Great job! Keep making progress.

Word of Caution

Please note since your story was formed to protect you, it will do whatever it takes to stay alive, including involving others. Now that you know one of the stories that has influenced your decision-making process, can you think of anyone else that shares your belief? That person may agree with you "men are dogs" after you were cheated on. Maybe they agree with you when you say "there's no getting ahead in this world" after you were overlooked for a promotion. Perhaps your story stays alive through your relationships. If your partner was unfaithful, do the rest of the men you date have to pay the price? Are you constantly looking for evidence of infidelity to the point you drive everyone away?

As the saying goes, "Misery loves company," and your story works the same way.

Think of at least one person that helps you validate your story.

_____

_____

_____

_____

_____

_____

_____

Next, write how this person helps you validate your story.

_____

_____

_____

_____

_____

_____

_____

_____

_____

_____

_____

_____

_____

How does validating your story hold this person back?

_____

_____

_____

_____

_____

_____

_____

_____

_____

_____

_____

_____

How else has your story impacted those around you?

_____

_____

_____

_____

_____

_____

_____

_____

_____

_____

_____

_____

Overall, how has this story affected your life, especially in the area of relationships?

_____

_____

_____

_____

_____

_____

_____

_____

_____

_____

_____

_____

At this point, you may want to speak to the person(s) that helps you validate your story and tell him/her how you are trying to improve your life. Maybe they will be supportive and even want to embark on this journey with you. On the other hand, there may be someone who, what can I say?..."old habits die hard," and they will not be able to help you. When speaking to that person if you find yourself falling into the trap of validating your old story, simply try to change the subject and move on.

To move forward, what actions do you feel you need to take in order to keep yourself from falling into the false perceptions your story left you with before?

_____

_____

_____

_____

_____

_____

_____

_____

_____

Now let's break these actions down. What action can you take immediately?

_____

_____

_____

_____

_____

_____

_____

_____

_____

_____

_____

What actions may take a little longer to complete?

_____

_____

_____

_____

_____

_____

_____

_____

_____

_____

_____

_____

Now that you have found the story that has clouded your vision, you do not have to suffer anymore. Use those painful thoughts and memories as motivators to really release your story once and for all. Hopefully, you will find yourself continuing to move forward and removing other harmful stories. Congratulations on taking control of your life!

CHAPTER 13

Creating Your Life Without the Story in Place.

Now is the time to start fresh. You should feel lighter now that you are not weighted down by your story. Try to surround yourself with positive influences in your life that will encourage you. If there are still a couple of naysayers, I will show you how to deal with them in the upcoming chapters.

In the meantime, take a walk down memory lane and think of all of the things you loved to do as a kid, anything from hobbies to simple things like riding your bike or hanging out with friends. Write down everything that comes to mind.

_____

_____

_____

_____

_____

_____

_____

_____

_____

_____

_____

_____

Now take a look at all of the activities you love to do now. Try to focus on the things you really get lost in where time flies without you even noticing it. List these things.

_____

_____

_____

_____

_____

_____

_____

_____

_____

_____

_____

_____

_____

Go back down memory lane and think about what you always wanted to do as a kid. What was your dream job and why? Really focus on the "why." What was it about that job that really appealed to you?

_____

_____

_____

_____

_____

_____

_____

_____

_____

_____

_____

_____

_____

What talents do you bring to the world? You may look at your diva list or what your best friend mentioned to refresh your memory. However, try to add even more onto the list. Really dig deep and do not hold back on all of those things that you are good at.

_____

_____

_____

_____

_____

_____

_____

_____

_____

_____

_____

Looking at the talents you listed, what tangible gifts can you offer to others? What are you good at doing or making?

_____

_____

_____

_____

_____

_____

_____

_____

_____

_____

_____

What activities could you do every day that you enjoy so much you could not think of not doing them?

_____

_____

_____

_____

_____

_____

_____

_____

_____

_____

_____

_____

_____

_____

What would you say on your deathbed that would reassure you that you led a successful life? State all of the activities and things you will have done that show you led a life of fulfillment, meaning, and happiness.

_____

_____

_____

_____

_____

_____

_____

_____

_____

_____

_____

_____

_____

What are your top five passions that you will pursue?

#1 _____

_____

_____

_____

_____

_____

#2 _____

_____

_____

_____

_____

_____

_____

#3 _____

_____

_____

_____

_____

_____

_____

#4 _____

_____

_____

_____

_____

#5 _____

_____

_____

_____

_____

After answering these questions, I hope it reignited some dreams from the past. Hopefully, other ideas popped into your head of new things you want to pursue too. The world is your oyster and you have the power of choice. All of us have hopes, dreams, and areas where we show talent. However, the difference between leading a successful and happy life is whether you make the choice to pursue these avenues or not. Of all of the items listed, I hope you have the confidence and make the choice to go out and DO at least one of them.

CHAPTER 14

There's No Time Like the Present.

If one of your dreams is to jump out of an airplane, I understand the odds are you don't have an airplane in your backyard at your disposal to do this. However, you can at least do a little research on the topic such as where do they offer such a service, how much does it cost, is there any prep work involved and so on. I would also suggest simply making a phone call. You might ask what it feels like to jump out of an airplane and other questions like this so you can get really pumped up for the experience. What it comes down to is there are a variety of ways to **get started right now**.

What can you do right now, no matter how small, to move forward in attaining your goal or passion?

_____

_____

_____

_____

_____

_____

_____

_____

_____

_____

_____

_____

Word of Caution: Watch Out for the Trap.

We have been so conditioned to postpone things that it will probably be the first thing that happens; you will find an excuse not to make that first step. These excuses can range from "they are probably not open" to "I'll wait until the kids go to sleep so they don't disturb me while I'm looking things up." When you are in the midst of the postponing process acknowledge it, then **move forward**. If it is midnight maybe the location is not open; however, you could leave a message so they can call you back. Take the time right then and there to look things up online. Make yourself a priority!

Re-Train Your Brain

After moving forward, be your biggest supporter. Turn off thoughts such as "I hope I'm making the right choice." Instead, think of how fun it is going to be or "I'm so glad I'm finally doing this." We know how powerful thoughts can be, and you certainly do not want negativity ruining your momentum.

Overcoming Negative Thoughts

The art of overcoming a negative thought is rather simple. Whenever you find yourself thinking of something that is not helpful, simply say "no," dismiss it, and think of something else. If you do this process enough times, your brain starts to get it and it will not go into those dark places.

In order to increase the positivity of your general outlook, make sure you post your passion cards and anything else that triggers positive feelings. Family photos of a great vacation, books you love, a picture or statue of something that brings a feeling of peace and serenity etc.... Surrounding yourself with things you love is always a great boost.

What are some things you can display around your home that will bring positive feelings to you?

_____

_____

_____

_____

_____

_____

_____

_____

_____

_____

_____

_____

Now is not the time to give up or postpone anything. You have made so much progress that you must move forward. Remember, if you are overwhelmed simply break that task down into smaller pieces. There are plenty of simple things you can do to keep moving forward. Do one thing on your list, acknowledge the progress made, and put the list away until the next day. It is amazing what a night's sleep can do. When you look at the list again, you may find yourself wanting to do several things on the list. Just give yourself the opportunity to grow and do not lose the momentum you worked so hard to attain.

CHAPTER 15

What Else Has Been Holding You Back?

Let's face it: in order to do something new, we all have had to step out of our comfort zone. Fear is never easy to admit. However, even though we may have been raised to be strong we all have a little fear in us, and sometimes the hardest thing to do is to admit that. It's okay to be afraid, and it's actually good to admit being afraid instead of trying to cover it up. Recognizing your fear is the only way to overcome it.

What are some fears you face now that you have established your goals or passions? State your fears for each goal or passion you listed.

#1 _____

_____

_____

_____

_____

#2 _____

_____

_____

_____

_____

#3 _____

_____

_____

_____

#4 _____

_____

_____

_____

#5 _____

_____

_____

_____

_____

_____

_____

_____

Whenever you are faced with fear, remember it is nothing but a negative thought that can be overcome by saying "no" to it, then moving on and thinking about something else—preferably what you would gain from completing your goal.

Let's practice this process:

Your response may look something like this:

Goal: *being a boss*

Positive: *getting a raise*

Negative: *I have to take charge and tell people what to do.*

Negative outcome: *I may have to boss some of my friends around and they may not like it.*

Implications of that fear: *I may lose some friends.*

Commitment: *I will talk to my friends after getting the promotion and tell them how I feel about my new position and how I do not want it to affect our friendship.*

Your turn:

State your first goal or passion you want to accomplish.

#1 _____

_____

_____

_____

_____

_____

_____

Write the positive result from attaining this goal.

_____

_____

_____

_____

_____

_____

_____

Write the negative result from attaining this goal.

_____

_____

_____

_____

_____

_____

_____

Why am I creating this negative outcome? What are you afraid of?

_____

_____

_____

_____

_____

_____

_____

Based on your response, what are the implications of that fear?

_____

_____

_____

_____

_____

_____

What is your commitment?

_____

_____

_____

_____

_____

_____

Do the same for goal/passions #2-5.

#2 _____

_____

_____

_____

_____

_____

Write the positive result from attaining this goal.

_____

_____

_____

_____

_____

_____

_____

Write the negative result from attaining this goal.

_____

_____

_____

_____

_____

_____

_____

Why am I creating this negative outcome? What are you afraid of?

_____

_____

_____

_____

_____

_____

Based on your response, what are the implications of that fear?

_____

_____

_____

_____

_____

_____

What is your commitment?

_____

_____

_____

_____

_____

_____

#3 _____

_____

_____

_____

_____

_____

_____

Write the positive result from attaining this goal.

_____

_____

_____

_____

_____

_____

Write the negative result from attaining this goal.

_____

_____

_____

_____

_____

_____

Why am I creating this negative outcome? What are you afraid of?

_____

_____

_____

_____

_____

_____

Based on your response, what are the implications of that fear?

_____

_____

_____

_____

_____

_____

What is your commitment?

_____

_____

_____

_____

_____

_____

#4 _____

_____

_____

_____

_____

_____

_____

Write the positive result from attaining this goal.

_____

_____

_____

_____

_____

_____

_____

Write the negative result from attaining this goal.

_____

_____

_____

_____

_____

_____

Why am I creating this negative outcome? What are you afraid of?

_____

_____

_____

_____

_____

_____

_____

Based on your response, what are the implications of that fear?

_____

_____

_____

_____

_____

_____

What is your commitment?

_____

_____

_____

_____

_____

_____

#5 _____

_____

_____

_____

_____

_____

_____

Write the positive result from attaining this goal.

_____

_____

_____

_____

_____

_____

_____

Write the negative result from attaining this goal.

_____

_____

_____

_____

_____

_____

_____

Why am I creating this negative outcome? What are you afraid of?

_____

_____

_____

_____

_____

_____

_____

Based on your response, what are the implications of that fear?

_____

_____

_____

_____

_____

_____

_____

What is your commitment?

_____

_____

_____

_____

_____

_____

_____

Now that you have addressed your fears for each of your goals or passions, you will feel better because what usually paralyzes us is the fear of the unknown. Identifying what your underlying fear of accomplishing your goal or passion is will help you move forward because you can take charge and face your fear. It will no longer keep you stuck or you can reevaluate your goals or passions effectively because you have the complete picture surrounding what you want. Make sure you use this tool whenever you have a big decision to make.

CHAPTER 16

The Art of Saying "No."

You have made some real progress! You have identified your story and you have determined what you want and do not want out of life. You have created in your mind a perfect day and have a clear image of what your life could be like. You have also made a commitment to really start living and letting others know how awesome you are. Additionally, you have learned how to interact with negative people and the importance of setting yourself free from things you have no control over. You also know the importance of surrounding yourself with positive people. Now that you have released your story from providing you protection, you are able to reevaluate your relationship with those who may try to help you keep your story alive and address the fears surrounding your goals and passions. However, one of your greatest accomplishments during your journey is embracing "there is no time like the present" and making progress toward your goal each and every day no matter how small. You have really accomplished a great deal!

Now onward and upward!

It's OK to Say "No."

When it comes down to it, there may be some people that will not be that enthusiastic about your new attitude toward life and the goals you have set for yourself. However, what you are doing is EXTREMELY important and you must do everything in your power to go for it, including saying "no" to others from time to time.

Here are a few different ways to get out of something other than flat out saying "no":

I would love to but I'm in the middle of something.

Wow, I would really love to help but I can't at this moment.

I've got so many obligations at this time, I'm going to have to take a pass on this one.

Wow, if you'd caught me sooner there would have been a possibility, but unfortunately I have another obligation.

Sorry, just can't do it. It's hard for me to say this but I hope you understand.

Think of a situation where someone asked you to do something and it really did not fit in your schedule but you did it anyway. Write down a way in which you could have said "no" to that person.

_____

_____

_____

_____

_____

_____

_____

_____

_____

_____

_____

_____

Now think of another situation where someone asked you to do something and it really did not fit into your schedule but you did it anyway. Write down another way in which you could have said "no" to that person.

_____

_____

_____

_____

_____

_____

_____

_____

_____

_____

_____

If someone gives you the "cold shoulder" or insults you, just say "I'm sorry you feel that way" and walk away. Sometimes people take advantage of others and it's difficult to lose their "go to" person. However, you are in control of your life, and in order to make things happen you must put your needs first from time to time.

What it comes down to is shifting control. You must take ownership for what happens in your life and not rely on someone else to make it better for you. Remember, you call the shots and you decide what you want to partake in or not. If you wait for someone else to make you happy, not only are you putting too much pressure on that person, you are slowing down your process immensely because you have to wait around for **them**. It's almost like getting a driver's license. Before you had your driver's license you had to wait around for Mom, Dad, or maybe your older brother or sister to give you a ride somewhere. I know I would think, *Geez, I could have been there and back by now*. Once you got that driver's license, think of the feeling it gave you. You could pretty much pick up and go whenever you wanted. Do that for yourself in your own life. Take control of your happiness and don't waste your time waiting around for others.

Although saying "no" may take some time to perfect, it is definitely something you want to practice. Saying "no" does not make you mean, it is just another way of releasing you from being the victim. If you find yourself doing something you really did not want to do, you have no one to blame but yourself. Give yourself the opportunity to enjoy life and make the most of your precious time.

CHAPTER 17

Positive Attitudes Are Good But BEWARE!

You have learned to think positively and how to take charge and I hope you are feeling pretty good about yourself; however, this is a time to really take note. Sometimes you may feel you are doing so well you stop moving forward. Beware of looking back and saying, "Look at all that I have accomplished already." Or "Well I've worked this hard for so long, I deserve a break." Statements like these can completely unravel all of the work you have done in a matter of days. I encourage you to take note of how your life has changed for the better; however, if you feel yourself losing momentum, acknowledge that feeling and then dismiss it. Next, do something that will move you closer to your goal. It doesn't have to be monumental, but do something to keep you on track.

Think of one thing you have attempted to do in the past you were unable to successfully complete.

_____

_____

_____

_____

_____

_____

_____

_____

_____

_____

_____

_____

Think of the reason(s) why your plans did not work out for you.

_____

_____

_____

_____

_____

_____

_____

_____

_____

_____

_____

_____

_____

Was there a "red flag" or a point where you could have done some-thing to get yourself back on track? Explain the situation.

_____

_____

_____

_____

_____

_____

_____

_____

_____

_____

_____

_____

Looking back, what could you have done to address the problem(s) before it completely derailed your plan?

_____

_____

_____

_____

_____

_____

_____

_____

_____

_____

_____

_____

When you are realistic about what is happening, you give yourself the opportunity to look at a problem before it derails you. Think of a lawn. If you keep looking at one patch of grass and do not look or take care of the rest of the lawn, before you know it you will have nothing but weeds to look at. Take the time to address problems before they become big ones. A minor setback is better than derailing your entire process.

CHAPTER 18

You Can Choose Your Friends But Not Your Family.

Who you decide to associate with can make all the difference in the world. When you have positive people around you who support your goals, you feel energized and ready to do more. When you have negativity around you constantly questioning what you are doing, putting down your progress, or giving you the "you're doomed and you're never going to make it" speech, it completely zaps you of precious energy. I know you may not be able to choose your family but, like your friends, you can choose to be around them or not. Please take note of who you decide to spend time with. If one or several of your friends keep trying to validate one of the stories you have released even after you have explained what you are doing and redirecting the conversation, it may be time to let that person go as a friend. However, it may not be that easy with family. Limit your contact with negative family members and perhaps make the decision not to share what you are doing if you know they will be critical.

If you are pretty secure a family member is going to question your changes and there is no way of avoiding it, play it out in your head.

Pretend you are facing the person that will most likely confront you. Write down all of the things that may come up during that conversation.

_____

_____

_____

_____

_____

_____

_____

_____

_____

_____

_____

_____

Next, think of what you can say to counteract these statements in a **calming** and **nondestructive way**. You do not want to "add fuel to the fire." Remember ultimately, they may never agree with what you are doing and you always have the option of walking away.

_____

_____

_____

_____

_____

_____

_____

_____

_____

_____

_____

If you choose to take part in the negativity and do not surround yourself with positive and supportive people, it may be easy to play the victim. By playing the victim, you may fall into the trap of giving up control. It can be so easy to blame others for your unhappiness and consequently completely derail your progress. Take charge of your life and choose to surround yourself with positivity.

When all is said and done, it all comes down to doing your best and only you know what your best is. If you are constantly trying to compare yourself to others or aspire to what others think "the best" is, you are fighting a losing battle. Give yourself the opportunity to succeed.

CHAPTER 19

The Past Is the Past.

Now that you have a complete "game plan" to living a happy and fulfilling life, it's time to finally let go of past negativity—choices with negative consequences, the hurt, and all of your past injuries. Harboring anger, like your story, eats away at you. It clouds your thinking and judgment and keeps you chained to unproductive ways. You also become so used to looking to the past that you lose sight of the present and the future.

When we lock people into places of disappointment or hurt, we never allow them the opportunity to become a positive influence in our lives no matter how hard they try. It takes so much energy to continue to stay mad at someone. They may do something kind and your body starts to experience the niceness, then you have to remind yourself about the incident that happened in the past and work yourself into that angry moment time and time again. When you dwell on the past, it keeps you from healing because you become the victim: "Look what they done to me!" Once you let it go, the past no longer has control over you.

To be perfectly clear, use experience as a learning tool; however, do not allow one lesson to affect your entire life and keep you from living life to its fullest.

Forgiveness

Forgiveness is the key to unlocking those chains and giving yourself the freedom to do whatever you like without the repercussions of those ugly thoughts of revenge or self-degradation. However, do not confuse forgiveness with condoning the behavior. It does not mean the situation never took place and therefore you cannot learn from it. It means everyone is human and sometimes people do things that are simply wrong. *Forgiveness is not holding on to the anger that surrounds the situation.*

Learning to Let Go

Think of one person you are holding a grudge against.

_____

_____

Think of what that person did to make you upset.

_____

_____

_____

_____

_____

Think of what you gain by holding onto that grudge. Dig deep and think of all areas of your life that are affected by holding onto that grudge.

_____

_____

_____

_____

_____

_____

_____

_____

_____

_____

_____

_____

Write a letter to the person you hold a grudge against, forgiving them. Remember, *forgiveness is not necessarily condoning the behavior, it is letting go of the anger surrounding the situation.*

_____

_____

_____

_____

_____

_____

_____

_____

_____

_____

_____

_____

Think of what you will be like now that you have given up the anger. How will that relationship be? How will it affect other relationships?

_____

_____

_____

_____

_____

_____

_____

_____

_____

_____

_____

Think of all of the activities and other things you will do now that you
have released the anger.

_____

_____

_____

_____

_____

_____

_____

_____

_____

_____

_____

_____

Not only is it good to forgive others, it is also good to forgive yourself. Use this exercise to forgive yourself for anything you may feel guilty about as well. Ultimately by choosing to forgive, you give yourself the opportunity to live life to its fullest because remember, there are no "do-overs," and you cannot make up for lost time.

CHAPTER 20

Happily Ever After!

Let's take a walk down "memory lane." You have done an extensive amount of work:

Chapter one focused on remembering who you were as a child and the happiness you experienced. You also looked into times when you were unhappy and how these times may have led to your story.

Chapter two focused on what damaging lessons you may have acquired and determining what your story was.

Chapter three focused on the power of your thoughts. You focused on what you would like your career, health, hobbies, home life, finances, and relationships to look like. You also determined what passions you want to pursue and how you want others to perceive you. Ultimately you determined what story you needed to release in order to achieve those goals.

Chapter four focused on the importance of releasing your story. You looked into what it would feel like if you did not pursue your goals or passions and whether or not you could follow your own advice.

Chapter five focused on what you are leaving behind for others. You had the opportunity to write two biographies—one where you lived out your goals and passions, and the other where you lived life on the same track you were on when you started the program.

Chapter six focused on looking at what you really want in your life and what you do not want in your life and determining what your top five goals or passions are.

Chapter seven focused on really living life and not just going through the motions. You chose a goal or passion, then identified the fear surrounding accomplishing it. You also found other ways to make comfortable strides toward your goal.

Chapter eight focused on creating the perfect life. You found that there are areas of your life you love as they are and there are areas that you would like to improve upon. More importantly, you found that it is okay to focus on other things from time to time as long as you do not lose yourself in the process.

Chapter nine focused on remembering your diva status. You brought forward all of the things you are good at also, the things you are appreciated and admired for. In addition, you took another look at achieving a goal you may have been afraid to pursue in the past.

Chapter ten focused on releasing yourself from any responsibility you felt from circumstances beyond your control. You also made your own mantra and passion or goal cards, which are hopefully hanging in your home now.

Chapter eleven focused on releasing your story and acknowledging you no longer need the protection your story provided.

Chapter twelve focused on acknowledging how others played a part in keeping your story alive. You found how to release them from that responsibility and how to keep yourself from falling back into your story trap.

Chapter thirteen focused on creating your life without your story in place. You looked at things you liked to do as a child and things you love to do now to help you secure a life full of success, meaning, and happiness. You also reevaluated your top five passions or goals.

Chapter fourteen focused on getting started on those passions or goals right now. You also found how to overcome negative thoughts and move forward no matter how small the task may seem.

Chapter fifteen focused on other fears that may be holding you back and how to overcome them.

Chapter sixteen focused on how to say "no." You found how important your journey is, it is okay to say "no," and several ways how to do it.

Chapter seventeen focused on how to have a positive attitude without it completely unraveling the work you have done.

Chapter eighteen focused on how to deal with negative family members who may not understand what you are doing. You also learned how to avoid becoming a victim.

Chapter nineteen focused on letting the past go. You learned forgiveness is not holding on to the anger that surrounds the situation and is the best option because it gives you the opportunity to fully live life again without pent-up anger or frustration.

Now that you have completed this journey, I hope you have a new outlook on life. I hope you feel like your dreams are possibilities and you have a game plan for accomplishing those goals and passions.

I also hope you see yourself in a different light. It is amazing how chained your story has kept you, and by releasing it your possibilities are endless. You are a tremendous person with a wealth of knowledge and gifts to offer the world. You offer value to each and every person you meet. You have the ability to "live out loud" and fully and wholeheartedly love yourself and others. By continuing to say "yes" to yourself, you have embarked on another amazing journey. The life you will lead now can encompass all you ever wanted and more. By using the tools, you have learned you have the ability to live life without limits. Your life story can resemble the one you wrote in which you accomplished all of your goals and dreams because you've already created that life in your mind. Remember, anything is possible because you now hold the key.

Congratulations on choosing YOU!